Ben Gadsby-Williams

PARKER
wants to fly

Illustrations by Volodymyr Hoshurenko

Pregnancy
Sickness
Support

Charity # 1094788

For Dad

Parker is his name, a happy little penguin.

But he couldn't help feeling he was missing something.

He had family and friends, of that he was sure.

But he set off alone anyway, in search for a cure.

Parker was walking along the ice one day.

When he spotted a bird and stopped to say.

"How did you get up there so high in the sky!?"

"With my wings of course!" was the birds reply.

"I have wings perhaps I'll try."

"Don't be silly!" said the bird "Penguins can't fly!"

Feeling upset Parker started to cry.

"I want to fly like other birds", he said with a sigh.

As Parker laid down on the ice for the night.

He started to dream what it would be like in flight.

With the wind in his feathers he'd soar through the air.
Flying faster and faster, as fast as he dared.

Early next morning with his dreams still nearby.

Today was the day he was going to fly!

He was planning on going as far as he could see!

But not too far… He'll be back for his tea.

"But how will I get up there!?" Parker frowned
"How will I get off this icy cold ground?"

Feeling brave and excited and full of hope.
"I've got it!" he said "I'll find a big slope!"

Parker searched far and wide for a slope that was good.

Then he saw one up high, where a familiar bird stood.

He climbed and he climbed till he reached to the top.

He was tired and scared "Oh my! What a drop!"

"What you doing up here!?" asked the bird.

"I'm going to fly!" said Parker undeterred.

To the edge he went nearer, to reach Parker strived.

As he closed his eyes tight he jumped then he dived.

Down Parker went always picking up speed.

"I'm going to make it! It's guaranteed!"

At the end of the slope there was an incline.

"This is it!" Parker thought, "My moment to shine."

"What was this feeling? This feeling quite rare?"

He opened his eyes, "Oh wow! I'm up in the air!"

Before he was able to enjoy his success.

Parker found himself troubled and in distress.

Down came Parker falling out of the sky.

The bird flew past him and squawked "Goodbye…"

He fluttered and he flapped with all of his might.

But he was losing the battle he was losing the fight.

Parker landed on his head with an almighty thump!

He rubbed it and wondered "Why on earth did I jump?"

"I told you!" said bird, "Penguins can't fly!"

Parker stood himself up, "Just watch me try!"

Parker continued to follow his quest.

What he saw then he would never have guessed.

He stood there in wonder, staring with delight.

For just over there was a magnificent kite!

Parker ran to the kite with blistering speed!
"Great!" he said, "it's just what I need!"

"Now I don't want to travel too far from home."
"I've got an idea, I'll tie the string to a stone."

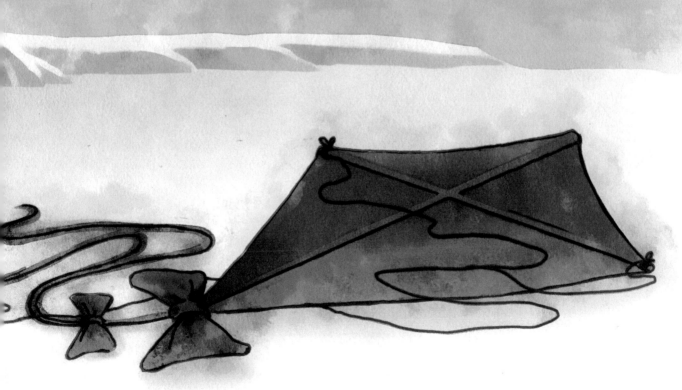

With the string tied tight he was ready to go.

He waited and waited for the wind to blow.

Then the wind blew strong with a mighty gust.

So Parker jumped in the air with an almighty thrust.

Up, up and up the red kite flew.

"Oh wow!" exclaimed Parker, "What a view!"

He saw his friends and his family, as clouds whizzed by.
But then he began falling, he didn't know why.

"What was that sound? That sound that went ping."
"Oh no!" Cried Parker! "That sound was the string!"

Then *that* bird came along he squawked and he spoke.

"Oh dear little penguin, looks like your string broke!"

Darting and swirling around and around.

Parker was falling, falling back down to the ground.

PING!

Then came that feeling, the one just like before.

Crashing down with a bump, back onto the floor.

Sitting on the ice and rubbing his head.

"I told you! Penguins can't fly", Again *that* bird said.

Parker cried then he fled.

Parker wandered the ice feeling hurt and alone.

Battered and bruised "If only I'd flown."

Looking down at his feet, Parker felt glum.

"Who could help me now? I know! My mum!"

"Mummy, Mummy I have wings but I can't fly."

"Mummy, Mummy please tell me why."

"My dear Parker haven't you heard?"

"You're more special than any other bird."

"Walk that way to the edge of the sea."

"Don't give up Parker, and soon you will see."

Parker walked as far as he his little feet could go.

Through the gusty winds, and through the white snow.

He walked and walked further than any time before.

His tired little legs carried him right to the sea shore.

Parker gazed at the water, this place that was new.

He'd never laid eyes on anything so big and so blue.

From way in the distance, was a voice Parker heard.

"Ha! Ha! Penguins can't fly!", again said *that* bird!

Not paying attention to the wind blowing stiff.

The rude bird was heading straight for a cliff!

Before he could swerve he hit the cliff with a smash!

Down he went tumbling into the sea with a splash!

Bird was troubled and hurt, he squawked with a yelp.
"Please little bird, I'm in need of some help."

Parker thought to himself "Oh no! What to do!?"

"*That* birds going to drown into that deep dark blue!"

"I really must save him I really must try."

"But to get over there I'm going to have to fly."

Parker ran and he flapped so fast that he slipped.

On the edge of the water he stumbled and tripped.

Parker was falling with his eyes tightly clenched.

The next thing he knew, he was totally drenched.

Laying in the water feeling pretty dim.

A peculiar feeling came over him.

He wasn't worried, frightened or afraid.

As his little tail moved and it swayed.

Fast across the water Parker was skimming.
To Parker's surprise, he found himself swimming!

"I've found it! That something that was missing all along!"
"This is just like flying! But in the water's where I belong!"

Swimming faster and faster, Parker shouted "It's great!"

"But I better go help *that* bird before it's too late."

Parker swam up to bird, still full of emotion.

Scooped him up with his beak, back out of the ocean.

"Thank you for saving me I thought I was fish food."

"I'm ever so sorry for being so mean and so rude."

"That's quite alright." Parker said with a grin.

"Did you see me just then!? Did you see me swim!?"

"I did little penguin! You're such a fast little thing."

"May I ask a favour? Would you help stretch my wing?

"Of course I will" said Parker, so he gave it a tug.

"That's done it!" said bird "by the way my name's Doug"

"My name is Parker, let's make amends."

As they shook wings politely,

knowing they'll soon be best friends.

And best friends they were, together they had so much fun!

Both flying and swimming towards the setting sun.

Ben Gadsby-Williams
Parker wants to fly

E-mail: Ben@recollectionmedia.com

ISBN-10: 1511420146
ISBN-13: 978-1511420143

72103384R00029

Made in the USA
Columbia, SC
12 June 2017